4/98

Animal Athletes

OLYMPIANS OF THE WILD WORLD

Animal Athletes

OLYMPIANS OF THE WILD WORLD

PHOTOGRAPHS BY

Frans Lanting

TEXT BY CYNTHIA BIX AND DIANA LANDAU

A WALKING STICK PRESS BOOK

published by

THE NATURE COMPANY

and

ANDREWS AND McMEEL

A Universal Press Syndicate Company

Kansas City

The Nature Company is dedicated to providing products and experiences that encourage the joyous observation, understanding, and appreciation of nature. Our goal is to kindle your sense of wonder and help you to feel good about the world in which you live.

Photographs and preface © 1996 by Frans Lanting
All other contents © 1996 by Walking Stick Press

Animal Athletes was prepared for publication at Walking Stick Press, San Francisco

Designed by Linda Herman
Edited by Diana Landau
Design associate, Joanna Lynch
Composition by Joanna Lynch and Miriam Lewis

Library of Congress Cataloging-in-Publication Data

Lanting, Frans.
    Animal athletes: olympians of the wild world/photographs by Frans Lanting; text by Cynthia Bix and Diana Landau.
        p.   cm.
    "A Walking Stick Press book."
    Summary: Provides photographs and text for a variety of wild animals, including the cheetah, emperor penguin, orangutan, and chameleon.
    ISBN 0-8362-2522-8 (hd)
    1. Animals—Juvenile literature. 2. Vertebrates—Juvenile literature. [1. Animals.] I. Bix, Cynthia Overbeck.
    II. Landau, Diana, 1950-   . III. Title.
    QL49.L327 1996   96-14388
    591—dc20   CIP

Page 1 photograph: An ostrich races across the Kalahari salt flats of southern Africa. This flightless bird—largest of all birds—depends on its ground speed to escape danger.
Frontispiece photograph: An impala doe bounds across the African plains.

Printed in Singapore by Tien Wah Press

To order this book or to learn the location of The Nature Company store nearest you, call 1-800-227-1114, or write The Nature Company, P.O. Box 188, Florence, Kentucky 41022.

Attention: Schools and Businesses. Andrews and McMeel books are available at quantity discounts with bulk purchase for educational, business, or sales promotional use. For information, please write to: Special Sales Department, Andrews and McMeel, a Universal Press Syndicate Company, 4520 Main Street, Kansas City, Missouri 64111.

First printing

Contents

The rare and endangered proboscis monkey inhabits the coastal mangrove forests of Borneo. These monkeys often make spectacular long jumps to cross tidal creeks.

Preface

The chameleon stretched himself forward until he hung on with only his rear legs and a tail curled around a branch. His eyes were focused on a grasshopper, clinging to a slender stem in the undergrowth of a rainforest in Madagascar. I crouched nearby with a camera, every bit as poised as he was. When he opened his mouth, ever so slowly, I knew he was taking final aim.

His tongue shot out so fast that I couldn't see what was happening. It was a rubber-band blur. But months later, when I studied the pictures at home, I marveled at the chameleon's precision. On film his long tongue was frozen in action, and I could see that, just as an Olympian archer would do, the chameleon had struck at the perfect angle.

Some people may be surprised by the idea of comparing animals to athletes. But I've looked at them this way for many years. As a wildlife photographer, I have documented animals in wild places from Africa to Antarctica. I've watched orangutans swing through the forests of Borneo; I've followed emperor penguins tobogganing across the Antarctic ice. In southern Africa, I hid by a waterhole for days on end, watching elephants wrestle and play in the shallows.

When you spend as much time as I do living and working

close to animals, you begin to understand that you can't take their amazing athletic abilities for granted. Yes, a cheetah is born with the body to run fast—but just like an Olympic athlete, it must train constantly to achieve a peak performance. Of course, there is a crucial difference. For the animals, running as fast as they can or leaping as far as possible are daily acts of survival.

In this book I hope to share the awe I feel for the strength, agility, and sheer power of the wild animals I photograph—and the kinship I feel when I'm among them. In my work I try to capture the moments that define an animal's life. Many of these moments occur at times when an animal displays its personal best—the giant bounds of impalas escaping a pride of lions, the grace of an albatross soaring over an oceanic gale. Even the intense concentration and skill of that chameleon in Madagascar, who hit the bull's-eye when he zapped his prey.

Frans Lanting
Santa Cruz, California

Cheetah

Champion of the Chase

Among all creatures on earth, the cheetah holds the land speed record. This long-limbed, elegant cat of the African plains is a short-distance specialist, timed at up to 68 mph for short bursts. Human athletes under their own power can approach such speed only with a big assist from gravity—on downhill skis, for example, or falling out of airplanes.

Like human sprinters, the cheetah's forte is acceleration. From a standing start it can be traveling 45 mph within two seconds—covering about 65 yards—and reach 60 mph in another few seconds. The cheetah needs to be quick off the mark, because the fleet gazelles that are its chief prey are almost as fast (about 62 mph). But, like humans who run the 100 meters, the cheetah can sustain top speed for only a few hundred yards. If it hasn't caught the gazelle by then, it probably won't.

A hunting cheetah in full stride is among the most stirring sights in the wild world. The cheetah's anatomy is perfectly designed for speed. Like most big cats, it has about 500 voluntary muscles—an amazing number for any mammal—and especially large and strong muscles in the legs, back, and feet. Long legs, relatively light bones, and an extremely flexible spine all help make the cheetah champion of the chase.

Our domestic animal athletes don't even come close to the cheetah's speed. A racing greyhound tops out at 39 mph; a thoroughbred racehorse at 47.5.

An animal's speed is determined by the length of its stride and how often it can complete a stride (frequency). All cats are well adapted for long strides, with a special stance (only their toes touch the ground), plenty of mobility in their shoulder blades, and long vertebrae between their ribs and pelvis, which allow the spine to flex. In cheetahs, these features are even more exaggerated than in other cats.

Africa's wide-open plains are the arena in which the cheetah and its prey stage their life-or-death contests. These cats are found in a

The cheetah's speed comes from the length and frequency of its stride, aided by its flexible spine and long, slender legs.

"Every part of the cheetah's body helps it to run fast. Keeping its head steady, the cheetah fixes its sight on the prey. As its long legs reach out, sturdy claws grip the ground. Both the claws and pads on the bottom of its feet keep them from sliding and help the cheetah change direction quickly. As it reaches full speed, its backbone bends and then extends, acting like a spring to propel the cheetah forward."

Caroline Arnold

Cheetahs have a more "doglike" shape than other great cats, and they hunt in the daytime, unlike most cats.

wide band of territory south of the Sahara, extending almost across the continent. The largest populations are in southern Africa—in Namibia, Botswana, and Zimbabwe. They once inhabited all the lands eastward to India, and there may still be a few in wilder parts of northern Iran, but no wild cheetahs remain on the Indian subcontinent.

People who share the cheetah's habitat have long admired its sleek looks and pursuit speed. More docile in temperament than other big cats, cheetahs were once tamed and used to hunt game, dating back to ancient Egypt. In India—before they became extinct there—they were taught to ride on elephants with their masters. The hounds would locate game, then the cheetah would leap down to make the kill. Among Arab tribes, fine horses bore them to the gazelle hunt. When not hunting they were treated like pets, playing peacefully with the children and dogs. Cheetahs have even been used to hunt coyotes in the American Southwest, though this is now banned.

Fortunately, keeping cheetahs as pets is now forbidden in many countries, the U.S. included. Joy Adamson, who became famous for returning the "Born Free" lioness Elsa to the wild, once adopted a young cheetah that had been raised as a pet. She taught Pippa to survive in the wild, too, and her studies of

Pippa and her cubs provided valuable information about the cheetah's way of life.

Adamson's book about raising Pippa describes the young cheetah playing a game of "tag" with a bold secretary bird and chasing an old football around, batting it with her paws like a soccer player. Sometimes she seemed to run just for the joy of it. "Once we reached the plain I let [Pippa] loose, and off she shot. It was wonderful to watch her effortless movements as she darted with lightning speed into the open."

Running may be the cheetah's claim to fame—but, like most cats, they spend much more time resting. Cheetahs are usually photographed lounging in the sun, sleeping off a meal, grooming their fur, or surveying the surrounding country from a perch such as an anthill or fallen tree. They love a high viewpoint where their keen eyes can scan for prey or danger. Cheetahs climb trees pretty well, though they are not really built for it. Their center of gravity is fairly high, and they have blunt, nonretractable claws—their most uncatlike feature. Only the dewclaws—located higher up on the paw like a thumb—are truly sharp, and a major weapon in hunting.

Cheetahs mostly live and hunt alone, though cubs stay with their mothers until they are full-grown. Also, young males may band together in temporary hunting parties—

Cheetahs use their keen eyesight to locate prey and keep watch for possible dangers—like lions.

so it's not ususual to see small groups of cheetahs. During the two years it takes for young cheetahs to mature, their mother devotes much effort to teaching them hunting skills: How to choose prey, how to stalk close to the quarry, and so on. She may partly kill prey and let the cubs finish it off, or capture and release small prey for them to practice on.

While many of Africa's great predators hunt by night, the cheetah is a daytime hunter. This may help it compete with lions, leopards, and hyenas. In hunting style, it shows traits of both the "courser" and the "stalker." Coursers—usually pack hunters like wolves and wild dogs—hunt by sight and chase their prey down, while stalkers—most cats—sneak up on it from hiding. Cheetahs do have some doglike traits, such as their long-legged build, but they don't pursue

Young cheetahs stay with their mothers until nearly full-grown, and must learn hunting skills from her.

Though not as social as lions, cheetahs are often seen together. Females and their young live together, and males may join each other in long-term hunting "coalitions."

prey over long distances. And they do stalk prey where the terrain has enough cover.

Cheetahs are highly efficient hunters, making a kill on more than half of their attempts (compared with the lion's success rate of 30 percent). Success is much more likely if the cheetah gets close to the quarry before starting its dash—within 60 yards. Its speed enables it to catch prey that eludes other hunters, but it can't handle very large animals. Wildebeest and Cape buffalo, for example, must be left to the lions. Cheetahs have to kill often and eat quickly. They stand in constant danger of having their kills stolen by those more powerful (lion, leopard) or more numerous (hyenas).

The chase itself is a matter of blurred seconds. As the cheetah reaches full-bore speed, all his genetic and learned skills are operating at peak. His tail stretches out behind for balance or acts as a rudder in the turns. Agile enough on his long legs, he still prefers a straightaway dash. Wildly zigzagging prey can sometimes escape or even make him fall. At the moment of truth, he reaches out his front paws and hooks a dewclaw into the animal's flank, then throws his weight into reverse—or simply swats it off balance. Even a little slowing allows the cat to leap forward and find his stranglehold.

> "The cheetah is a glorious hunter—in that flash of spotted gold one sees an animal performing what it has evolved for thousands of years to do so well...."
>
> Cynthia Moss

Even though cheetahs are excellent hunters and bear large litters in the wild, they are seriously endangered today. They rarely breed in captivity, for one thing. In their native lands, hunters once killed thousands for their beautiful skins, and poachers still break the law to shoot them. And as game animals become scarcer, cheetahs face more competition from other predators—more of their kills are stolen and more cubs killed.

Their ideal habitat—the open plains—have been largely taken over by human herders and their cattle. This forces cheetahs into rougher terrain, where their hunting style is less effective and injuries more common. Like human athletes, a cheetah with even a slight injury is badly handicapped, as it depends so much on speed.

Cheetahs are even threatened in the parks and reserves that are supposed to protect them. The cats are likely to be found in parks—the landscape is right for them and hunting is banned. But since they are active in the daytime, they are easily spotted by safari tourists and guides. While trying to get close for photos, tourists may harass cheetahs or interrupt their hunts.

The cheetah is endangered by many factors, mainly the loss of its preferred habitat.

Worldwide efforts are under way to preserve cheetahs in the wild, including educational programs that bring hand-raised animals into school classrooms. The Cheetah Conservation Fund recently acquired a farm in Namibia where they can do long-term behavior and breeding studies on cheetahs. If these efforts succeed, the spotted sprinter will win its race for survival.

A Zulu legend explains why cheetahs have those distinctive black marks curving down from their eyes. A lazy hunter, observing a mother cheetah hunting, decided to steal one of her cubs and teach it to hunt for him. But the greedy man took all three cubs, leaving the mother cheetah heartbroken. Though the hunter's village later punished him and returned her cubs, she had wept so much that the tears permanently stained her face.

Emperor Penguin
King of Cold-Weather Endurance

People brave the cold to take part in difficult tests of endurance such as cross-country skiing, dogsled racing, winter diving, and polar expeditions. But no creature is as good at coping with cold weather as the stoic emperor penguin, the endurance champion of the bird world.

At the bottom of the world stretches the continent of Antarctica—a frozen land of endless snow and harsh light, of jagged ice formations and treacherous crevasses. As the howling Antarctic winter sets in, nearly every living thing hurries off to more hospitable climes until spring. But one hardy creature will not only stay all through the winter, it will actually breed and raise its young. This is the emperor penguin.

This cold-weather champion leads a double life. In the sea, it is a master swimmer and deep-diver. On land, it treks long distances on foot over rough terrain to reach its breeding grounds.

In March—the Antarctic autumn—emperor penguins emerge by the thousands from the surrounding seas, where they have been swimming and foraging all summer. The sea around the continent has begun to freeze solid, forming a vast ice shelf (or "fast ice") hundreds of miles wide, at its edges.

In single file, the penguins begin a long march—up to 100 miles—inland across the new ice to their traditional nesting place, called a rookery. Their journey, like that of a cross-country skier or biathlete, requires great endurance and an ability to "read" the rough and unpredictable terrain. The penguins must hop between chunks of floating ice and cross deep crevasses that can be deceptively covered with snow.

The emperors' short legs are fine for swimming but can make walking slow and clumsy. When walking and hopping simply become

> "These birds clearly possessed a dignity all the more pronounced because of their bulk, and when they walked it was with a regal gait, measured and slow, the heads dipping from side to side."
>
> Doug Allan

A colony of emperor penguins at their rookery in the Antarctic springtime.

too slow and slippery, or when they want to get down slopes quickly, the emperors use a technique called "tobogganing." They throw themselves flat on their stomachs, push with their feet and flippers, and zip along over the ice at an amazing pace. It looks a lot like sledding—without the sled. Once they reach the rookery, these hardy birds will mate and lay their eggs in the dead of winter—in blizzards, 100-mile-an-hour winds, and temperatures dipping below minus 70 degrees Fahrenheit.

The emperors' unique natural history demands this life of extremes. They must breed in winter in order to produce offspring with a chance to survive. Their young are slow to develop and can't come to maturity in the very short Antarctic summer. So their strategy is to produce eggs in midwinter, which hatch in late winter. Then by midsummer, when conditions are milder and life is easier, the chicks are ready to head out to open water.

Special body features, as well as behaviors, protect the emperor and help it to survive. It is the largest of penguins, standing 3½ feet tall and weighing up to 80 pounds. Its round,

"When they come to crevasses, they know which to cross and which to skirt. The odd thing is that there is often no apparent difference in the strength and thickness of the one they take with confidence and the one they bypass. But the emperors know what they are doing. …Their road is a sure one."

Jean Rivolier

A procession of emperors treks back to the rookery after a fishing expedition to the open sea.

"By the time just about every creature bigger than a mite has left Antarctica for the winter, these penguins get out of the water and march *inland*—sometimes more than 100 miles. This aerial view shows their tobogganing form."

Frans Lanting

A group behavior called "huddling" helps the emperor survive. The males in the rookery—as many as 12,000 of them—stand close together with their backs to the stinging snow and wind. They shuffle around continuously, so each gets a turn in the warm middle.

compact body has a two-inch-thick layer of insulating fat, or blubber.

Like all penguins, the emperor has a dense coat of feathers. Stiff, curved outer feathers overlap each other closely; each has a base of down for insulation. Every feather has small muscles attached it, so that the feathers can be held out straight to trap an insulating layer of air. In the water they can be flattened, so the bird is watertight and streamlined for swimming.

Once the penguins arrive at their rookery and winter sets in, they need all the protection they can get. After a male and female mate and produce a single egg (usually in May), incubating it becomes the male's responsibility. He rolls the egg onto the top of his feet and covers it with a flap of abdominal fat.

The female immediately sets off for the open sea, many miles away, to replenish her resources by feeding on fish and squid. For the next two months, the faithful male will stand with the egg on his feet—through the dark Antarctic winter days and nights, in blinding blizzards, without shelter or food.

Digging in with their feet and bracing with their flippers, emperors can "toboggan" on flat ground or even up a slight grade.

At last, with what one observer calls "nearly magical timing," the females return from the sea just as the chicks begin to hatch. By the time the chicks are about five months old, spring has come to Antarctica. Most of the temporary fast ice has melted, so it's a shorter hike from the rookery back to the open sea.

Like all penguins, emperors are sleek, fast swimmers and expert divers—far different from the portly waddlers they become on land. They "fly" along underwater, propelling themselves with their powerful flippers and using their feet and tails as rudders. They are capable of swimming up to 9.5 mph for short distances.

The emperor is the champion diver of the bird world. Although it usually makes a series of quick dives when hunting fish and squid, one researcher has reported a record dive of 500 meters (1,640 feet) deep. (The record for a human diver using SCUBA gear is 475 feet deep.) The emperor can stay under water for as long as 18 minutes, although most dives are closer to four or five minutes.

At home in two worlds—the icy sea and the frozen, blizzard-swept land—the emperor is impressive not only for its size and power, but for its staunch spirit in the face of one of the earth's most challenging environments.

A pair of unrelated adults and their six- to eight-week-old chicks.

Orangutan

Jungle Gymnast

On the Southeast Asian islands of Borneo and Sumatra lives a creature that the Malay people call *orang utan*, which means "person of the forest." Scientists call this shaggy, redhaired great ape *Pongo pygmaeus*. (*Pongo* is an African word for ape; *pygmaeus* means "short.") And because he is so superbly equipped to make his way in his rainforest home, an expert says with admiration: "In the great forest, orangutans are the masters of the universe."

This member of the primate family is built for a life in the trees. Its body shares some of the traits of the male gymnasts we watch performing feats of strength and control on the rings—hugely developed back, shoulder, and arm muscles; relatively long arms and short legs; and big, strong hands. With its massive arm and shoulder muscles and its incredible strength and flexibility, the orangutan is the gymnast *par excellence* of the Indonesian rainforests.

The orang's arms are incredibly long—about two-thirds of its body length, which in males is up to 4½ feet tall. Its short legs are as flexible as its arms. In fact, with toes that work like fingers, it really has two pairs of arms and hands. Both hands and feet have very long, curved fingers that act as hooks when the orangutan hangs onto a vine or a branch.

This "equipment" allows the orangutan to weave its way through the rainforest canopy, 70 feet or more above the

Orangutan specialist Biruté Galdikas spent many days slogging through the Bornean forest while studying her subjects, and vividly describes the advantages of their arboreal life: "Tangled vegetation closed in around me, impeding movement. Small vines grabbed at my ankles and tripped me, hurling me against the hard points of the knee roots....Watching the imperious passage of the orangutans up above, I felt like an odious, incompetent worm, crawling laboriously in the undergrowth...."

A young female orang-utan streaks through the trees—aiming a slap at Frans Lanting along the way! Holding on with just one hand and one foot, she is totally in control.

Completely at ease upside-down, a subadult (left) and a younger orang "hang out."

ground. For this animal, says photographer Michael Nichols, the jungle is "full of highways, with limbs and vines for trails in the lower canopy."

Unlike monkeys and other smaller primates, orangs rarely let go and leap from branch to branch without holding on. Instead, they use a technique called "brachiation" ("brachial" refers to arms). Using branches and trailing liana vines, the animal swings along hand over hand, its legs dangling. Some primates that brachiate make a few pumping swings, working up momentum to carry them to the desired next branch—like a person on a playground swing trying to get as high as possible. Often the orang makes progress by grasping a branch with one hand, then a leg, then the other two limbs. Or it may just dangle comfortably while eating fruit or leaves.

Young orangutans move quickly and gracefully through the trees, but adults are often too heavy for vigorous swinging—especially the males, which can grow to weigh 300 pounds. Frans Lanting says, "They're so heavy, they have to be careful. They live in familiar 'neighborhoods,' so they probably know the best way to get from Tree A to Tree B…which branches to use." Adult males—usually twice as big as the females—must spend more time on the ground.

An adult male feeding up in the trees will avoid branches too small to support him. To get at the fruit and leaves he wants, he may settle in a comfortable spot and simply pull the tree branches toward him with his powerful arms, stripping food from them before letting them go.

The male orangutan is an impressive figure of legendary strength. Victorian naturalist Alfred Russel Wallace reported that local people believed the orang could kill a crocodile with its hands. They said, "There is no animal in the jungle so strong as he."

When they're about five or six years old, adult males begin to develop their distinctive fatty cheek flaps. These reach their full development when the male is mature, at about age 15. (Orangutans in the wild are believed to live about 40 years.) The males also have an inflatable throat sac which they "pump up" in preparation for emitting a loud roar that can be heard echoing through the forest over a half mile away.

The roar is usually issued as a warning to other males who may try to encroach on an adult male's territory. Except for the times when they are mating, males generally live alone. In fact, all orangutans live a more-or-less solitary existence—they don't form troops or family groups like most other primates.

By day, individual orangs roam over a fairly small home range of up to three square miles. They spend nearly all of their time feeding—after all, it takes an enormous amount of food to sustain such a large body! This may help to explain why they live alone. Because food is widely scattered and sometimes scarce, they must spread out. A group of these big eaters would soon wipe out the food sources in a given area.

Basically vegetarians, orangutans feed on about 400 kinds of fruit and other foods. Their sharp teeth and large, strong jaws easily penetrate tough peels. They also eat a variety of leaves, bark, sap, funguses, and insects. As Galdikas says, "Wild orangutans spend up to eight hours a day munching, chomping, processing, bending, picking, sorting, and devouring foodstuffs."

After a day of searching out food—with occasional rests in between—orangutans prepare for the night by building a nest in the trees, bending and breaking branches into a kind of platform. They make a new nest each night. Orangutans apparently don't like rain, and often they fashion a leafy roof over their nests.

> "The long call of the adult male orangutan never ceases to impress me...It is the loudest and most intimidating sound in the Bornean rain forest. The long call lasts at least one minute and sometimes as long as four minutes....From what people have told me, an orangutan long call equals or even surpasses a lion's roar in volume and intensity."
>
> Biruté Galdikas

Although orangutans are usually solitary, mothers keep their babies with them for several years. The relationship between mothers and offspring is very close. The infant is born not knowing how to find food or how to move through the trees—it must learn these skills from its mother. She remembers where certain fruits can be found at what times of year, and she shows her offspring how to open and eat them. She also coaches her baby patiently until it learns how to swing along through the canopy.

By about age four, juveniles begin to seek out playmates and gradually—especially the males—move farther and farther away from the mother. Female orangutans usually give birth to a single baby every seven to eight years. This low birth rate, combined with about a 50 percent rate of infant mortality, means that orangutan populations are in danger of dwindling.

The Malay natives who called orangutans "persons of the forest" were responding to some of the very human qualities these gentle, intelligent, forest-dwelling apes possess. Orangutans' faces, mostly hairless like our own, are highly expressive. They bare their teeth and stare when threatening. An open mouth with teeth covered indicates readiness to play. They also seem to feel emotions such as fear, jealousy, and sadness. The mothers' attachment to their young is strong, and they have been observed to mourn over a dead infant, grooming and carrying its body around for a long time before abandoning it.

These highly intelligent creatures, so close to humans in their physical characteristics and gestures, are in grave danger of disappearing, along with the rainforests that are their home. The tiny range where they still exist is shrinking due to logging and clearing of land. Besides the destruction of their habitat, orangutans fall prey to poachers who cruelly kill the mothers and kidnap the infants for sale to private collectors.

Long-term research by biologists such as Biruté Galdikas has shown the way toward saving these gentle creatures. One pioneering program shelters orphaned young orangs, who are taught by humans—standing in for their mothers—how to climb and swing on networks of rope "vines." Such rehabilitation and breeding programs will help to save the orangs from extinction, but preservation of their natural environment is essential if they are to survive.

At a rehabilitation center in Borneo, orphaned young orangutans are taught to climb and swing on ropes, and gradually return to life in the wild.

Impala

Hurdling to Survival

A lioness crouches in the tall grass, her eyes fixed on a herd of impala grazing nearby. The great cat inches slowly forward. The impalas' heads fly up. Their sensitive noses sniff the air. Suddenly, as the lioness moves toward them, the impala explode into action. They leap 10 feet into the air as if propelled by springs, then in all directions—forward, sideways, even over each others' backs.

Confused and unable to cut one animal out from the rest, the lioness loses her moment. The herd dashes off, bounding easily in great, 35-foot-long leaps over the broken terrain. This time, at least, the cat will go hungry.

The impala and the lioness are a perfect example of what ecologists call the "coevolution" of species. Over the ages, pursuit by lions and other predators honed the impala's impressive speed, agility, and leaping skills, so that the fittest of its kind were able to survive and reproduce. At the same time, lions had to become exceptionally strong, stealthy, and well-armed to catch their antelope prey and keep their own species in existence. The two creatures are so well-matched that often an impala's leap will save its life only by inches, Frans Lanting notes.

The quick, graceful impala is among the most beautiful of all the antelopes that roam Africa's vast landscapes. Long-necked and slender-legged, this medium-sized, hoofed mammal is related to creatures such as the gazelle, the gnu, and the waterbuck, but is not exactly like any of them.

Human jumpers and hurdlers have much in common with the impala. An impala can certainly outleap even an Olympic high-jumper. The best human athletes can clear about 8 feet, and that's with a running start. But both human and animal depend on a combination of leg muscles—especially heavily muscled thighs—and long tendons that serve as "springs." Good jumps depend on speed and a fast takeoff. Bending the legs and then extending the muscles at takeoff, combined with the elastic action of the tendons, give height to a jump.

A young impala buck completes a leap in classic style, forelegs outstretched, hind legs tucked high for safety, and white tail flared in alarm.

Mopane woodland in the Kalahari is a good example of the mixed habitat impala favor.

The impala's glossy coat is reddish-brown or chestnut with a white underside; distinctive black stripes run vertically along its tail and haunches. The male sports elegant ribbed horns, curved in a lyre shape; in fact, impala means "lyre horn" in Greek.

Not a fighter, the impala's best defense against predators such as lions, cheetahs, leopards, and hunting dogs is a combination of alertness, social organization, choice of habitat, and incredible athletic ability.

The stage on which the drama of chase and capture is enacted is a patchwork of landscapes throughout eastern and southern Africa. Impala favor open woodland areas—places with scattered trees and light bush—rather than either dense woodlands or open plains. They often stay in "edge" areas where two kinds of vegetation come together—where grassy plains meet the woodlands, for example.

In these edge areas, the impala finds a variety of plants to eat, as well as cooling shade during the heat of the day. It also gains some protection from predators. At night, a herd of impala will often move deeper into the brush, where the big cats can't creep up on them without making noise that betrays their presence.

During the dry season, the impala must also be near a source of water, usually a waterhole that it shares with its fellow inhabitants of the African savannah—elephants and giraffes, rhinos and zebra, as well as predators.

The impala is ever alert, always on the lookout for predators. All its senses—especially its sense of smell—are acute. Its eyes, located on the sides of its head, have elongated pupils, so the animal can see out of the corners of its eyes even while grazing. Whenever a predator does appear, the impala herd reacts in a unique way that demonstrates both their social organization and their amazing athleticism.

Even while she feeds, this doe stays alert. Her large ears can swivel forward or back to pick up sound, and her eyes can see nearly 360 degrees.

At the first sign of danger, the herd suddenly explodes into action. Antelope expert C. A. Spinage vividly describes the scene: "When a herd of impala explodes into leaping, jinking confusion, it is not a wild panic reaction, but certain action patterns are repeated each time. Thus each leap appears to be oriented towards other members of the group: magnificent leaps of three meters in height and over 11 meters in length, often passing over the back of another.

These high-jumps are followed by a last high kick with the hind legs as the forelegs touch the ground; so high indeed are they that the animal nearly somersaults."

Like other antelopes, impala communicate a lot by scent, which is released from special glands on their hind legs or feet. One purpose of their leaping around may be to alert one another by releasing the "alarm" scent from glands on their feet. Impala, as well as other antelopes, also stamp the ground when danger threatens, probably to release this scent.

Another possible reason for the way they leap around is to display their black-and-white rump and tail as a warning signal to the herd. The impalas' alarm behavior may also confuse a predator, so it can't effectively single out an animal from the herd.

If a predator gives chase, the impala can run, too. Although it can't keep running at full speed for very long, the impala is a marvel of grace and fleetness on the short sprint. Streaking over the ground on its long legs, it often stretches its body out full-length in spectacular leaps that carry it over rough terrain. Like a hurdler who must take hurdles at full stride in a race, the impala can easily clear obstacles such as bushes or rocks. If its pursuer can't jump the obstacle, or must slow down to do so, it loses precious time—and probably its

The impala's athleticism comes partly from its long legs, which increase the length of its stride and therefore its speed. It also has great stability when running. Its split hooves splay apart when they land, so its feet won't sink or dig into soft ground. And its leg bones are made in a way that prevents the leg from moving sideways, so there is less risk of the impala losing its balance at top speed.

meal. Sometimes, at the critical moment when a lion or wild dog draws close and reaches out to strike, the impala leaps for its life—just far enough to escape.

The herd's social lifestyle is also closely tied in with the cycle of courtship and mating. Usually the female impalas form herds of 50 to 100. As soon as the males, or bucks, are old enough to leave their mothers, they join "bachelor herds" made up of bucks of varying ages.

The impala is a strongly territorial animal. The most powerful, or dominant, bucks establish their own exclusive areas where no other bucks can trespass. During mating season, a buck will collect a group of females and round them up, or "drive" them into a harem group, which he defends from other bucks. If another buck tries to challenge the dominant male, the defender will warn him off in a variety of ways. One of the oddest of his warning signals is a yawn. He may also "roar"—not like a lion, but with a noise more like a loud wheeze or snort.

Most social animals avoid all-out fights whenever possible. Serious injuries or deaths may be harmful to the whole herd or pack. Instead, they work out their conflicts with ritual behavior, showing dominance and submissiveness in ways that are understood by all members of their tribe. Impala bucks will fight one another as a last resort—even then, they do a lot of feinting and jabbing with their magnificent horns but don't usually hurt each other. If one contestant doesn't back down, however, he or the other buck may be badly hurt or even killed.

Impala sometimes face danger from each other, and always from predators. But as adaptable, hardy animals that live very successfully in their environment, they remain abundant on the savannahs of east and southern Africa. Yet the impala are affected by the same forces that currently touch all of Africa's wildlife—the growth of human population and competition for land. As more and more land is taken up for farming and raising livestock, the impala may be crowded out along with other wild animals—including those that prey on it. For now, these graceful animals wander and graze freely over the African landscape that is their home.

A full-grown impala buck displays his magnificent horns and superb musculature.

Dolphin

Swift Swimmer, Deep Diver, Aerial Acrobat

"As the shark approaches, the school tightens…the porpoises swimming so close to one another that fins and flukes almost touch. The school moves faster and faster through the water, swimming as a precision unit, breaking free in low-angle leaps. After a few minutes the school slows, prompted by the outlying members, who sense that pursuit has stopped and that they are once again safe."

This is how dolphin expert Ken Norris imagines a group of bottlenose dolphins (once called porpoises) escaping from a shark who has scented a newborn calf in their midst. His words describe some of this animal's chief characteristics—its cooperative social life and its great athletic ability in the water.

Dolphins are familiar to us from movies and water shows, in which they are usually star performers. Because they are such intelligent, adaptable creatures, dolphins of some species can be trained to do tricks that people find thrilling or amusing. As a result, they have also become a symbol for the rights of wild animals to live free and uncontrolled by man. But if we look deeper than the dolphin's entertainment value, or what it stands for, we find an animal whose life in the wild is one of nature's most fascinating stories.

Dolphins and whales are marine mammals, relatives in the order Cetacea (from the Latin word *cetus*, which means whale). All cetaceans have rounded, streamlined bodies, front flippers for steering, and a broad, powerful tail that propels them through the water with up-and-down strokes. All breathe air through a blowhole at the top of

Novelist Herman Melville, author of *Moby Dick*, probably had common dolphins in mind when he wrote, "They always swim in hilarious shoals which upon the sea keep tossing themselves to heaven like caps in a Fourth of July crowd."

A spinner dolphin surfaces, exhaling through its blowhole. Its elongated body, with pointed nose and flippers for steering, allows it to knife through the water at high speed.

The dolphin's extremely smooth, hairless skin secretes a polymer that bonds with water, decreasing friction as it moves through the sea.

their heads, and nurse their young, like other mammals. But beyond those basics, cetaceans can vary from the 5-foot-long Hector's dolphin to the enormous blue whale, the world's largest living creature at up to 90 feet long and 160 tons.

The dolphin's streamlined shape enables it to reach swimming speeds of up to 20 mph—not as fast as some fish, or even a few of its whale cousins, but very fast for a marine mammal. They are as quick as they need to be to catch the fish they prey on, and to escape predators that attack them—most often sharks or their own close relative, the killer whale.

Within the family Delphinidae, there are 33 species of "true dolphins." Hector's is the smallest, and the killer whale (orca) the largest, full-grown males reaching up to 29 feet. The ones we think of as "typical" dolphins are the pelagic, or open-ocean species, such as the common, bottlenose, spinner, and dusky dolphin. But dolphins inhabit all the world's oceans, from the polar regions to the equator, as well as harbors and freshwater rivers.

The remote ancestors of present-day dolphins and whales were land ungulates—hoofed animals—that probably ventured back into the water 45 to 60 (maybe even 70) million years ago, when mammals were just starting to multiply. One group apparently headed for the rivers, swamps, and estuaries that abounded in this early world. Exactly why, no one knows—food and safety were likely factors—but these were the forerunners of our dolphins and whales.

Cetaceans have senses specially adapted to the watery world they evolved in. Their sense of smell is practically nonexistent; instead, dolphins and whales taste and analyze the water surrounding them with numerous tongue papillae (taste buds), getting information this way much as land mammals "read" scents in the air.

Most cetaceans have good vision. Their eyes are specially constructed to see clearly underwater as well as in air. They can distinguish objects precisely—witness the accuracy of captive dolphins who pluck small fish from a trainer's hand while leaping from the water. Slow-motion film shows that they actually make subtle body corrections in mid-leap.

Touch is extremely important to dolphins. Their skin has countless nerve endings sensitive to the varying pressure and movement of water around them. This gives them a keen awareness of objects and other creatures nearby—how close, how large, how threatening—important in hunting prey, and in their social and mating behavior.

In the realm of sound and hearing, dolphins are supremely capable. Sound travels well through water, so this sense has a natural advantage. As social animals, they use a large repertoire of sounds, including squawks, cries, clicks, and whistles to convey anger, warning, distress, and probably pleasure. Every bottlenose dolphin has a "signature whistle" by which others in its school can identify it.

Clicks often combined into complex "click-trains," which sound to us like squeaky hinges or rasping whines. Click-trains are the sounds they use in "echolocation"—a kind of sonar that brings dolphins detailed information about each other and their environment. They send out ultra-high-frequency click-trains that bounce off objects around them, and listen for the returning echoes. This gives them a "sound picture" of the object: its size and shape, how far away it is, even the speed and direction of potential predators or prey. Some dolphins may stun their prey with bursts of echolocation clicks.

As early as the seventeenth century, naturalists noticed that dolphins had large brains in relation to their overall size. Brain size usually indicates intelligence, and dolphins display intelligence in other ways, too. They can adjust their behavior to different conditions, and they are good learners. They form complicated social relationships, which means that they must communicate with each other. This in turn makes it easier for humans to communicate with them. "Their friendliness toward humans stems from their sociability in nature," says Berndt Würsig.

"The dolphins like all whales are derived from an early stock of ungulates. Watch the undulations of a swimming dolphin, the backbone waving up and down as it beats the tailstock, and that action resembles very closely that of a galloping horse or wildebeest."

Berndt Würsig

Berndt Würsig describes how bottlenose dolphins hunt: "They seek schools of fish, and when they find one, they surround it, at times hitting it from different sides at precisely the same moment. Dolphin maneuvers can be highly coordinated, appearing almost premeditated or at least well practiced, with some individuals pushing the prey toward shore while others—in front, behind, above, and below—prevent their escape. A good game of soccer or polo, with each player knowing his or her position and role, comes to mind."

Cooperation is vital in many aspects of dolphins' lives. In an environment where danger can come from any direction, it's a great advantage to live in an organized society, where if just one member spots a predator, it can broadcast an alarm to all.

Schooling enables dolphins to track and catch prey more effectively. Though they are highly capable predators on their own, many dolphins have developed strategies for coordinated hunting that vastly increase their efficiency. Orcas, for example, herd herring into large roundish clumps, then swat their tails against the mass of small fish to stun them, providing a leisurely meal.

Dolphin societies are basically matriarchal—young female dolphins usually stay in the home ranges of their mothers and grandmothers. Males are more likely to roam farther, joining or visiting other schools. Females bear a single calf every three to six years. Calves are quite large and well developed at birth, because they must travel with the school almost immediately. As the young grow, they may be nursed or looked after by other females in the school.

Intelligent, socially oriented, and physically fit animals tend to engage in play—and dolphins are a prime example. As Frans Lanting notes, the dolphin lifestyle works so well that they often have excess energy and brainpower to burn, so they keep themselves stimulated by various forms of play.

Humans have provided dolphins with one of their favorite entertainments: riding the "bow wave" created in front of a boat or ship as it ploughs through the water at speed. Unless they have been regularly hunted or captured in an area, dolphins will usually race to intercept any boat they spot nearby, and position themselves barely ahead and to the side of the bow. There they glide along, without even needing to swim, in the pressure wave created by the boat's forward motion—sometimes leaping free of the water and falling back, sometimes changing places with other dolphins.

Many of us have seen dolphins playing and performing in water shows. But dolphins in the wild play without any human encouragement. The athletic feats most often observed by

people are those they perform above the water's surface—aerial acrobatics such as breaching, spinning, and all kinds of leaps: high, low, or twisting.

The spinner dolphin, which lives in Pacific waters around Hawaii, is well-named for its spectacular trademark move. As it leaps from the water, it spins rapidly along its full length, rotating up to six times before splashing back down. The dusky dolphin, a coastal resident of the southern oceans, common around New Zealand, is among the most energetic and acrobatic leapers. Once started, it may make 50 or 60 jumps before stopping.

The dolphin's swimming speed is legendary, but speed in the water can be deceptive. Reports of dolphins keeping pace with Navy ships making 40 knots (about 48 mph) led researchers to conduct speed trials with trained dolphins. It turned out they were not as fast as once thought—the Pacific bottlenose can swim up to 20.5 mph, and the spotted dolphin nearly 28 mph. Of course, they can keep up with ships going much faster by riding bow waves.

All these feats are made possible by the dolphin's marvelously adapted body. Their shape is extremely "hydrodynamic" (as a

A beluga dives below the surface. Special adaptations in cetaceans permit deep diving.

Dolphins swim in a shallow lagoon. Since there is less resistance in air than in water, leaping out of the water ("porpoising") helps them maintain speed.

bird's wing or a race car is said to be aero-dynamic). That is, it presents the least possible resistance to the passage of water around it. All external body parts that might block the smooth flow of water—such as ears, sex organs, and teats—are flush with the body's surface or hidden within slits in the body wall. Breathing through the blowhole at the top of the head allows cetaceans to exchange air without interrupting their smooth swimming motion.

"We leaned over the rail to watch about a dozen of them station themselves alongside...riding effortlessly along below the surface....Occasionally one spun over and away from us in a graceful underwater barrel roll, to rise and "blow" a dozen yards away, outside the ship's bow wave. As quickly, another swung in to take its place. Occasionally one rose directly in front of our onrushing bow, sometimes blowing just before its smooth, shiny head broke the surface....All the movements of these magnificent animals showed exquisite and subtle response to the dense liquid around them."

Ken Norris

Whales are the undisputed deep divers among cetaceans. Sperm whales have been tracked by sonar to depths of more than a mile and a half, during dives lasting an hour or more. While dolphins don't dive as deep or as long, their dives have been measured as deep as 1,550 feet and up to eight minutes in length.

To dive so deep and for so long, cetaceans' bodies must be far more resistant to the effects of water pressure than ours are. Human divers suffer from painful "bends" or may die if they exceed strict limits on depth and length of time underwater. Various adaptations in whales and dolphins prevent the absorption of nitrogen into the blood at depths (which causes the bends). Their bodies also conserve oxygen during prolonged dives, and they can tolerate more carbon dioxide in their lungs than most nondiving mammals can.

People have felt a strong bond with dolphins for thousands of years, regarding them as kindred spirits in the seas. Their grace, intelligence, and high spirits have fascinated us, and we have long tried to know them better. Dedicated researchers have learned much about these amazing creatures, and much remains to be learned.

In the last few decades, we have also made progress toward ensuring that dolphins are safe from hunting and accidental death in fishermen's nets. But some species are still seriously endangered and most suffer to some extent from human impact on the seas, in the form of pollution, net-fishing, and illegal killing. The health of our watery planet and all its inhabitants depends on humans learning to cooperate and work together, at least as well as dolphins do.

Flying Frog
Glider in the Treetops

In 1869, the British naturalist Alfred Russel Wallace was tromping through the rainforests of Borneo when a local man brought him a surprising animal specimen. It was a large tree frog that Wallace later described as having "come down, in a slanting direction, from a high tree, as if it flew."

Wallace was fascinated. Examining the frog, he found "the toes very long and fully webbed to their very extremity, so that when expanded they offered a surface much larger than that of the body." He concluded that this was the first known case of a "flying frog."

These frogs don't truly fly, as birds or bats do. What they do is glide—somewhat like humans piloting a hang glider. In hang gliding, the pilot jumps off a cliff or hilltop and sails through the air at a gradual downward slant, held aloft by lightweight "wings" strapped to a harness. The pilot controls the craft by shifting his or her weight, or by changing the angle of the wings.

Flying frogs do much the same thing. With powerful hind legs they launch their lightweight bodies from a high branch into the air. They spread out their large webbed feet and hands, as well as special flaps of skin on their legs and arms. These membranes of skin act like miniature parachutes to slow the frog's descent.

Some flying frogs glide as far as 40 or 50 feet as they descend by stages from the treetops to vegetation lower down. For these little animals, gliding is an energy-efficient way to get quickly from one place to another. By moving its legs or twisting its toes, the flying frog can even turn as it glides, so it can land to the right or left of its original direction of launch.

The tree-dwelling creature Wallace found was one of the largest of the Bornean "flying" frogs. These include Wallace's flying frog (*Rhacophorus nigropalmatus*), the jade tree frog (*R. dulitensis*), and the frog pictured on these pages, the harlequin tree frog (*R. pardalis*).

A Bornean flying frog, its foot webs stretched wide for a parachute effect, glides down for a soft landing on a fern.

Borneo's forests are home to quite a few "flying" creatures—more than any other rainforest. The giant red flying squirrel (some as big as a house cat) glides as far as 425 feet between the trees on flaps of skin that stretch out along its sides. There are flying geckos and even flying snakes, which glide by swiveling their ribs to flatten out their bodies. One of the best reptile gliders is the "flying dragon"—a lizard about 8 to 10 inches long that can unfurl "wings" of skin to glide about 66 feet from one tree down to the base of another.

The world in which these airborne frogs make their home is the rich and varied rainforest of Borneo, a large island that is part of Indonesia. Here, huge trees reach 100 feet into the air. Their leafy tops meet and mingle in a dense umbrella of green, casting the forest floor, or understory, into dim green shade. Up in the sunlit canopy thrives a colorful community of fruits and flowers, birds, animals, and insects—some of which never come down to the ground. Up here the fly-

Aerial view of the rainforest canopy. Trees are spaced quite widely, so the flying frogs may glide up to 50 feet.

ing frog finds plenty of insects to feed on, and plenty of moisture from the frequent rains that fall on the canopy.

Like other tree frogs, the flying frog is uniquely adapted for its arboreal life. Its feet have large, round toe pads that help it climb and cling to vertical surfaces. Though many people assume that these pads adhere by suction, they actually have tiny specialized cells that can penetrate microscopic cracks and irregularities in tree trunks and branches. The pads also have glands that produce a sticky secretion to help the frog hold tight— sort of like the "stickum" that football players once used to catch passes.

The frogs' long legs also aid in climbing; the strong hind legs propel their leaps through the trees. Their large, well-developed eyes help them navigate through the canopy and track down insect prey. Scientists believe frogs have good depth and color perception, as well as the ability to see in all directions at once. They can spot an insect's slightest movement, even in the dark.

Frogs have a unique ability to regulate their body temperature by changing the color of their skin. Because the tree frog endures greater extremes of light and temperature than its pond-dwelling relatives, it can change even more than other frogs. Light

Visiting the ground during breeding season, a frog gets a rain-shower while resting in a mushroom cap.

The flying frog's skin performs many functions. Instead of drinking water, frogs absorb it through thin skin on their abdomen, called a "pelvic patch." And besides breathing through their lungs, they draw in oxygen and release carbon dioxide through their skin. To do this the skin must stay moist, a job performed by mucous-producing glands. The mucous also gives the skin a slippery film that protects against bacteria and helps the frog give predators "the slip."

colors reflect heat, so the frog's skin may get lighter in hot, bright sunshine. When temperatures drop or when it gets dark, the frog's skin grows darker to absorb warmth. These changes are caused by the movements of various pigments within the skin cells.

Color changes also provide camouflage. In response to signals from its hormones or nervous system, the frog's color may change to match that of the mottled brown bark or the bright green leaf it's sitting on. Then predators such as owls or monkeys are less likely to see it. If one does spot it, the flying frog can often glide to safety.

One of the few times the little frogs come down from the canopy is to breed. Their eggs, like those of all frogs, must hatch near water where the tadpoles can begin their development into adult frogs.

The flying frog is a fascinating example of an animal that has taken its family traits to extremes in adapting to its special environment. With its parachute-like feet and extra-streamlined body, it swoops through the rainforest canopy while other frogs make their way along the ground and through the water.

But like all inhabitants of the world's rainforests, the flying frog faces the threat of displacement from its natural habitat. As more and more forest is cleared for human

Flying frogs cling to tree trunks and other surfaces with their large feet and round, sticky toe pads.

With its slender body and long, strong hind legs, the flying frog is well equipped for life in the treetops.

use, and as the effects of pollution trickle into what forest is left, the frogs may face an uncertain future. One of only about a dozen kinds of flying frogs in the world, this agile creature is a valuable member of the rainforest's community of wonders.

African Wild Dog

Marathon Hunter of the Plains

Africa's hoofed animals must contend with some of the world's most powerful predators: lions, leopards, cheetahs, and hyenas. But the meat-eater most likely to scatter an antelope herd on sight is smaller and less fearsome-looking than any of these. It is the African wild dog—or more exactly, a pack of wild dogs.

Two main factors—endurance and teamwork—make the wild dog such a successful hunter. Though not very big themselves—about the size of a German shepherd—they can kill much larger animals like zebras by hunting in packs. And while a fleet gazelle might outpace them in a sprint, wild dogs can run and run, and then run some more—up to four or five miles at over 30 miles per hour, without tiring. Their prey cannot keep up such speed for as long. These dogs are the marathon runners of the African plains.

The African wild dog (also called the African or Cape hunting dog) is a distinct species. It's related to other wild canines like wolves and jackals but has some unusual traits. A medium-to-large-sized dog weighing 55 to 75 pounds when full-grown, the wild dog is noted for its boldly patched or spotted coat. Each dog has a unique coat pattern that probably helps them identify each other when far apart. Most have a white tip on their tails—a good way to keep track of the dog ahead when traveling through tall grass.

Wild dogs have amazingly large, round ears, which may aid in pack communication and locating prey. Long, lean but very muscular legs carry them

Technically, of course, wild dogs don't run marathons. The official distance of a marathon race is 26¼ miles. It's highly unlikely the dogs would chase anything that far. However, packs may well cover 20 or 30 miles at a stretch when out patrolling their range. Speedwise, they beat us handily. In the 5,000 meters—about as far as wild dogs chase their prey—human champions manage just over 14 mph, compared with the dogs' 30 mph.

A wild dog pack heads off into the African dusk on its nightly patrol.

on the chase. A short, broad muzzle with powerful jaws is their only real weapon—unlike big cats, who have claws that can slash and grip.

Wild dogs can live in many kinds of habitat—the grassy plains, or savannah, hills covered with dry vegetation, or open wooded country. They once populated nearly every part of Africa except the dense forests. Their range is much more limited today, because there are fewer prey animals and the dogs themselves have been ruthlessly hunted. There are some in South Africa, and some as far north as Ethiopia and Sudan.

Except when they have young pups, wild dogs are nomads. They patrol large home ranges that average 200 to 600 square miles, and up to 1,500 square miles. This species is not really territorial—that is, they don't "stake out" their turf and defend it against other wild dogs. Packs may mingle and overlap within their ranges, and even join each other on hunting forays.

Wild dogs live in places that are extremely dry for much of the year. They are very well adapted to this lifestyle, and can go for several days without water. Recent studies explain how this physical trait enables them to run long distances in hot climates. A network of blood vessels in their large ears helps in cooling off.

The wild dog's lean, long-legged frame combines speed and endurance.

Often called the "wolves" of Africa, wild dogs are very social animals, like their northern cousins (and just about all dogs). The pack is not just a temporary get-together for hunting prey, it is the focus of their whole lives. Members of a pack travel together, hunt and eat together, raise their pups cooperatively, and sometimes even feed each other as adults. They communicate vocally with an intricate vocabulary of squeaks, whines, hoots, and birdlike twittering sounds, and use body language as well.

Most often there are about 6 to 15 wild dogs in a pack. In former times, before hunting drastically reduced their numbers, packs were much larger—up to 40 dogs was fairly common. The more dogs, the better their chances for catching large prey, so as packs shrink in size, so does its range of potential

Still alert after a hard chase, a panting dog cools off in a waterhole.

food sources. The male dogs in a pack are usually related to each other, while females leave the pack at about age one-and-a-half to join other families of males. (This is the opposite of lions, where the "pride" is composed of female relatives and the males must leave to find a new pride.)

As in wolf packs, each wild dog has a different status in the pack. Some are more dominant: making decisions, leading hunts, bossing other dogs around. Others are more submissive: they let the "top dogs" dominate them, but they in turn dominate those that rank lower in the social order. There are actually two such rankings in a pack, separate ones for males and females.

Wild dogs cooperate in many ways to care for pups and their mothers. A pack often has a favorite breeding area within its vast range, and returns there when it's time for a female to give birth. She typically bears a litter of seven

In one pack observed by naturalists, a mother dog died when her pups were 5 weeks old, but the males of the pack continued to care for them and feed them by regurgitation until they were old enough to travel on the hunt.

Fanned out to cover as much ground as possible, a pack seeks prey by sight and scent.

to ten pups, but up to 15! Birth takes place during the dry season, when game is concentrated around waterholes. That way the dogs don't have to travel as far to make their kills.

The female shelters her young in a den, usually one abandoned by a warthog or aardvark. While she is unable to hunt, the pack will feed her by regurgitation—they gulp down big chunks of meat at the kill, travel back to the den, and bring the food up from their stomachs. This is how pups are fed, too, once they start eating solid food. Later, the mother may go on the hunt, leaving other dogs to "babysit" the pups.

Once the pups are old enough to venture outside the den, all the adult dogs are eager to greet them, licking and nudging and carrying them around. Females without pups of their own may try to "adopt" a pup. As the pups grow, they can be a nuisance to the older dogs, playfully attacking their tails as they rest—but a meaningful look or a swift kick is usually enough to send them scurrying.

Wild dogs hunt "at the edges of the day," as Frans Lanting notes—usually at dawn and at dusk. One pack member will sense that the time has come, get up from its resting place, and go over to greet and pass the word to another. One by one, each dog is greeted, until all are up and moving around excitedly. This pre-hunt ritual is called a "pep rally."

One dog—often the dominant male—may take the lead as the pack sets off, or several may lead. While seeking game, they move at a fast and purposeful trot that eats up the miles. In open country the dogs fan out horizontally to cover more territory; through dense vegetation, they travel single file. They seek their prey by sight, mostly, jumping up high now and then to see over tall grass. When they spot possible prey, they approach, still trotting, to about

A small herd of springbok antelope, favored prey of wild dogs, flashes white rump patches in an alarm signal.

The wild dog is one of world's most efficient predators. Zoologists judge this by observing how many times the animals chase prey, compared with how often they actually make a kill. Wild dog hunts are successful about 85 percent of the time.

500 yards away, then slow to a walk and fall into single file, heads low to the ground. This allows them to get as close as possible without spooking the prey.

But if an antelope or gazelle or wildebeest has spotted the dogs, its herd will be instantly alert. No other predator, not even a lion, inspires as much respect in its prey. They know their survival depends on keeping distance between them and the dogs, and will typically flee before the dogs can approach closer than 100 yards away—sometimes when they are still a half-mile off.

Sooner or later, one nervous beast will break into a run. The prey's flight triggers the dogs' chase reflex, and the deadly pursuit is on. A couple of possible scenarios can follow. The dogs may make one or more "test chases," which allows them to observe which animals might be the easiest targets. They may start out after more than one animal, and then break off less promising chases to join the one that seems likeliest to succeed.

The chase goes on relentlessly. Usually one dog stays in the lead, with a few others close behind and rest strung out in back. As the prey tires, it often begins to zigzag in desperation, but the rear dogs move up and "cut the corner" to prevent its escape. Contrary to some reports, the dogs don't run in relays, but this intercepting tactic can make it look like they do. If the prey tries to double back, there are always dogs in the rear to cut it off.

The kill is not a "clean" one, like a lion breaking the neck of its prey. After the first dog gets a grip or knocks the animal off balance, the others swarm over it and tear into its flesh around the vital organs. Often they start eating before the prey is fully dead, but shock probably spares it from feeling much pain. Still, the apparent savagery of wild dog kills has prejudiced people against them. Hunters and herders have felt justified in killing wild dogs on sight, almost anywhere. But this is a human value judgment. The dogs are making their living the way nature has equipped them to—and who are we to say which deaths are more "cruel" than others in the natural world?

Unlike lions and other social predators, wild dogs rarely fight over their kills. The pups are allowed to feed along with adults. If the kill is small and mostly eaten before they arrive, they'll be fed by regurgitation, as will any handicapped members of the pack who can't keep up. The dogs' willingness to share food this way keeps down conflicts around kills.

These tireless runners and team hunters are becoming scarce in most of Africa— there may only be a few thousand left on the whole continent. Ranchers and herding tribes have always killed them to protect their cattle, and hunters and game managers shot thousands, supposedly to protect the herd animals. But we now know that wild dogs, like wolves, help keep the size of game herds in balance with the ability of the land to feed them all.

Diseases like distemper and anthrax take their toll, and so do injuries. If a dominant dog is crippled by a kick from a zebra, the hunting success of the whole pack will suffer. In some places where they are scarce, the dogs are genetically weakened by inbreeding. But studies are under way to track the movements of wild dog packs. This will help us understand what it will take to keep these marathon hunters racing across the plains.

Members of a pack taking a midday rest.

Laysan albatrosses soaring above Midway Island in the Pacific. Albatrosses can stay aloft for months at a time.

Albatross

Sailor of the Skies

Dipping and wheeling, riding the wind above vast rolling seas on its outstretched wings, an albatross in flight is an awe-inspiring sight. A champion sailor on the air, this great seabird flies with effortless grace. Like an expert human sailor, the albatross takes advantage of every nuance of wind, water, and currents to make its way over the ocean.

This remarkable bird is one of the world's greatest long-distance fliers. Through calm weather and howling storms, the albatross glides over the open ocean for months at a time, without ever touching down on dry land. It can stay aloft almost continuously during the daylight hours—often even sleeping on the wing—yet it never seems to tire.

The distances albatrosses journey are mind-boggling. One albatross traveled almost 10,000 miles on a single trip before returning to the nest where his mate was incubating their egg. Once a young wandering albatross leaves the place where it hatched, it may circle the globe time after time, but somehow manages to return to that exact place six to twelve years later, to breed. Frans Lanting once calculated that a single albatross could cover five to ten million miles over its lifetime!

The secret of the albatross's legendary power to stay airborne lies in its wing structure. Its wings are exceptionally long and narrow. The wandering albatross has the greatest wingspan of all birds—up to 11½ feet—yet its wings are only about six to nine inches wide. In flight, these extraordinary wings perform like those of a glider plane, allowing the bird to ride wind and air currents without using valuable

Most of the 13 albatross species—including the huge wandering albatross—live in the Southern Hemisphere, from the edges of the Antarctic north to the Tropic of Capricorn. Only three species—the black-footed albatross, Laysan albatross, and short-tailed albatross—are found in the Northern Hemisphere, all in the Pacific Ocean.

energy flapping its wings. The wings can also be "locked" in the open position by a special arrangement of muscles and bones, so the albatross can fly on a kind of automatic pilot—probably even while sleeping.

Albatrosses also have an inborn knack for riding the wind. When traveling *with* the wind, the albatross can glide effortlessly along. When flying *into* the wind, it "tacks," zigzagging back and forth across the wind to move forward—much like a sailboat guided by an expert skipper.

When tacking into the wind, the albatross takes advantage of the difference in wind speed at the ocean's surface and above it. At about 50 feet above the water, the wind blows faster than at the surface, where friction slows it down. But there are also handy upcurrents of wind along the waves.

The dipping, wheeling flight pattern of an albatross riding these air currents is thrilling to watch. From aloft, it swoops downward, moving faster and faster, toward the water's surface. Just above the water, it swings around into the wind, one wingtip pointing down, the other up toward the sky. Upcurrents of air above the waves give it a boost and it rises, gathering speed, until it's ready to swoop and dip again.

Repeating this flight pattern over and over, the albatross can cover hundreds of

The albatross's long, narrow wings work like those of a glider plane.

Young albatrosses gather on a beach for wing-stretching exercises in preparation for taking off.

The albatross's whole body is perfectly adapted for life at sea. The bird can drink the ocean's salty water because of special glands above its eyes that remove excess salt from its body. This is released through short, tubular nostrils at the top of its bill. (In fact, the family of seabirds to which albatrosses belong is called Procellariiformes, which means "tubenoses.")

miles in a day without tiring, at speeds up to 50 miles an hour. Scientists have been able to trace the flights of individual birds using signals sent by radio transmitters attached to the birds and tracked by satellite.

The albatross's skillful flight techniques not only work extremely well, but these graceful birds often seem to swoop through the air for the sheer joy of it. Mildred and Harvey Fisher, who spent years observing albatrosses on Midway Island, wrote: "They obviously enjoy being in the air, and they fly even when they aren't going anywhere in particular."

Staying airborne for long stretches of time and covering enormous distances are essential to the albatross's survival. It's an offshore feeder, with a diet of mostly small squid, which are widely scattered over the vast open oceans. An albatross must range over miles and miles of water to find the best feeding areas. And when it has a chick to feed, an enormous amount of squid is called for—perhaps a dozen for just one feeding. To raise a chick, some albatrosses make 50 or 60 round-trip foraging expeditions, each about two days' travel. Others may range thousands of miles.

The albatross isn't a diver—it feeds from the water's surface. Scientists know that the birds forage mostly at night, when the squid, crustaceans, and fish they eat come to the surface. To feed, the albatross must come in for a landing on the moving swells. It lifts its wings and spreads its tail and big webbed feet to brake itself.

Albatrosses have learned that they can get an easy meal by following ships. Sometimes they stay around for days at a time. In fact, for centuries mariners have been amazed by the sight of the great birds following their ships for miles, far from any land. Yet sailors didn't always respect the albatross, and often killed them for meat or for sport. Noting their clumsy waddle when walking on the ship's deck, they nicknamed them "gooney birds" and "Mollymawks" (from Dutch words meaning "foolish gull").

Albatrosses are at their clumsiest when learning how to fly—a skill they must master through trial and error. Youngsters don't even begin to learn until they are three to nine

Adults in an albatross colony watch over a chick as another bird brakes for a landing.

These mysterious birds have inspired awe and wonder, fear and superstition. Some thought they were the souls of sailors who had been washed overboard, and they came to believe it was bad luck to kill one. In "The Rime of the Ancient Mariner," a famous poem by the English poet Samuel Taylor Coleridge, a sailor who shoots an albatross brings a terrible fate down upon himself and his whole ship.

months old. The chicks are born on the same nesting site where their parents and their parents before them were born.

At the age of four to twelve years old, depending on the species, a young albatross finds its way by instinct back to its place of birth. Now it is ready to choose the mate it will often keep for life. (They live at least 30 years, and some species as long as 80 years!) After a unique and complicated courting ritual of dance and sound, a couple eventually mates and cooperates to build a mounded nest on the ground.

All species lay a single egg, which takes up to 80 days to hatch. During this time, the parents take turns incubating the egg, while the unoccupied parent makes long journeys over the sea to find food. When the chick hatches, it spends up to nine months in its parents' care. During that time, the parents must continue their long food-gathering quests. They store the food in their stomachs and regurgitate it to feed their ravenous offspring.

Finally, the youngster is ready for flight training. Large groups of young Laysan and black-footed albatrosses exercise their wings, looking a lot like an aerobics class. Then they practice takeoffs and landings over and over, their clumsy attempts often ending in a dunking or a crash landing.

Once the chick leaves its birthplace, it will live for the next four to twelve years on the open ocean, until it is time to return to its breeding place and begin the cycle anew.

Although albatross breeding colonies are now protected by law around the world, the birds do face some threats out at sea. They may become entangled in fishing lines or swallow plastic objects floating on the water. The wandering albatross is especially affected by this. In some areas, humans fishing for squid may reduce the amount of food available.

Even in the remote parts of the world's oceans, humans must take care, so that these master sailors of the skies can live their lives free and wild, flying over the sea on any winds that blow.

And a good south wind
    sprung up behind:
The Albatross did follow,
And every day,
    for food or play,
Came to the
    mariners' hollo!

Samuel Taylor Coleridge
The Rime of the Ancient Mariner

Young African bull elephants butt heads in mock combat. Play fighting
can turn serious when they start competing for mates.

Elephant

The Spirit of Play

Some things about elephants are obvious: They're big, they're strong, they have a marvelous "fifth limb" called a trunk, and some have tusks and huge, floppy ears.

Thanks to the work of scientists who have lived in the wild with elephants, we now know many more fascinating things about these giants. Not only are they big and strong, they're also playful, funny, sensitive, expressive, affectionate, and highly intelligent. In fact, their great strength may be part of the reason why elephants have been free to develop the playful side of their character.

The whole idea of athletics, for people, grew out of natural, spontaneous, joyful movements of the body. Later these were organized into various team and individual sports. Top athletes know it's important, even while competing to be the best, to keep the spirit of play in what they do—to have fun. Animals, too, use their bodies in ways that are purely playful. The more intelligent the animal, the more likely it is to play just because it feels good, and to play with others of its kind. Elephants, as we've learned, are both intelligent and very social beings.

Elephants are the largest living land animals. A full-grown bull, or male, can be as tall as 13 feet (3.9 meters) at the shoulder and can weigh as much as 16,500 pounds, or about 8 tons (7,500 kilograms). Elephants this large belong to the species *Loxodonta africana*—the African elephant. This species lives on the savannahs of east, west, and central Africa. The African elephant has huge, fanlike ears and a sloping forehead. Both bulls and cows (females) have long, curved tusks.

The Asian elephant, *Elephas maximus*, is found in forested areas of India, Thailand, and parts of Southeast Asia. This species is generally

> "Elephants seem to realize that winning or losing doesn't count—the play's the thing. When animals of unequal size spar in play, the larger one often kneels to adjust its height to the smaller one."
>
> Stuart L. Brown

Safe between its mother's legs, a very young elephant calf bends to drink.

smaller than its African cousin, with a humped back, smaller ears, and a bulging forehead. Only the bulls grow tusks.

 The strength of elephants is legendary. They can easily uproot a small tree or break off a large branch with their trunks. Because of their strength and intelligence, they have been trained to do heavy labor in Asia for centuries. Even today, elephants still do logging work in places where machinery can't go. A single elephant may haul teak logs weighing as much as three tons up a steep slope, then lay them neatly in piles using its trunk. Captive elephants have been used to haul railroad cars and other equally big loads.

If an athlete is performing her best, people say she's "at the top of her game." As Frans Lanting says, the elephant is a creature who's "on top of its environment." As the biggest, strongest animals in their world, adult elephants face few threats from any predator except humans. Within their close-knit herds they interact constantly and often intensely with one another, expressing themselves with their bodies and a variety of sounds. The mostly peaceful rhythm of their lives allows plenty of opportunity for just "fooling around."

Baby elephants, or calves, like the young of most species, are especially playful. They charge each other and roll around in the dirt; they even make mock charges at birds or calves of other animals such as buffalos. Play is important for healthy physical and mental development in animals and humans alike. Experts describe three basic patterns of animal play: (1) play-fighting and wrestling; (2) high-spirited kicking and leaping, as lambs or antelopes do; and (3) playing with objects like rocks or sticks. All these kinds of play are a rehearsal for later life, as well as a way for young animals to establish relationships and learn about their surroundings.

Young bulls often play with each other by staging mock battles—butting heads, wrestling with their trunks, and clashing tusks. This kind of play is one way that they establish a "pecking order" among themselves and practice for the real conflicts they will have as full-grown bulls, competing for the right to mate with females.

Elephants may also play with people—at least those they know and trust. Douglas Chadwick describes Joyce Poole and a young bull elephant playing a game of "catch" with a buffalo chip. And there are many stories of zoo elephants playing with their handlers. Despite their massive size, elephants are

Writer Douglas Chadwick describes a visit to elephant researcher Joyce Poole, who studies elephants in Kenya's Amboseli National Park: "A twenty-year-old female…was soon racing around camp, trumpeting, head-shaking, ear-flapping….What had inspired all this? Joyce replied, 'She's just feeling playful.'" Poole goes on to say, "I'll be winding up a string used to mark out a vegetation study plot….So everyone has to trumpet and scream and race around. Then they all have to talk about it. And pretty soon one is winding the string up around its trunk. Then one whirls and winds it around all four legs. Then off they go into the bush, playing, hauling off all my string along with them. Nearly any other animal would have sniffed once at the string and gone on its way."

anything but clumsy. In fact, they have superb body control and can move with great delicacy—as in the familiar circus trick where an elephant gently rests a hoof on its trainer's prone body. In a close encounter with wild elephants, Frans Lanting recalls their "noiseless footfalls" as they stepped carefully over the stretched-out cords anchoring his tent.

Play is just one of many forms of communication among elephants. Every part of the animal's huge body, from its trunk to its tail, can express its emotions and intentions.

The most unique and expressive part of the elephant's body is its trunk. This remarkable organ has many uses—it's a nose, lips, arm, and fingers all in one. The trunk is extremely strong, yet sensitive. It contains no bones; instead it is all muscles—more than 50,000 of them. Some control "large-motor" activities like lifting or pushing heavy objects; others are for "small-motor" tasks needing precision control.

The elephant can use its whole trunk like a powerful arm; yet the flexible tip can grasp a single piece of fruit. An elephant often picks up a stick with its trunk and uses it as a tool to,

"When they bathe, elephants give every sign of thoroughly enjoying the experience, thrashing around in the water and often completely submerging themselves. The youngsters, in particular, show great high spirits, tussling with each other and climbing over the recumbent bodies of their elders."

S. K. Eltringham

An elephant uses its trunk like a snorkel while moving through deep water.

Elephants roughhousing in the water. Their great bulk makes them quite buoyant.

scratch itself, or just plays around with it. Of course, the elephant's trunk has practical, survival-oriented uses. All food is gathered with the trunk, then stuffed into the elephant's mouth. A thirsty elephant sucks up water partway into the trunk and squirts it into its mouth.

Elephants seem to love being in the water and are good swimmers. When bathing, they use their trunks to throw water back over their bodies. They also use the trunk as a kind of snorkel, holding its tip above the surface when moving through deep water.

The elephant's sense of smell is acute. With its trunk held high in the air, the animal can scent danger from far away. It passes the tip of its trunk over the ground or shrubbery—sometimes even over a human being—gathering information through scenting.

A large gathering of elephant clans crosses the Chobe River in Botswana.

The trunk is also important in communication. When they greet each other, elephants touch the tips of their trunks or even put them in each other's mouths to exchange information. They are very affectionate animals and often caress each other with their trunks. A mother touches her baby with her trunk to comfort or reassure it. And play among elephants often involves wrestling with their trunks.

Family members are very attached to one another. They come to each other's aid in times of sickness and danger, and reassure each other often by gentle touching and vocalizations.

After a separation, their reunions are exuberant and intense.

Elephants use a variety of sounds to "talk" to each other. Loud, trumpeting calls usually express excitement or agitation. They make rumbling noises and utter growls when they are feeling peaceful—or, in a different situation, when they are angry. Their repertoire includes a variety of squeaks and squeals, gurgles and roars. Recent studies reveal that elephants also communicate by "infrasound"—frequencies so low that humans can't hear them. This explained certain behaviors that had puzzled researchers—for example, why a herd in flight may split into two groups heading in different directions.

Long-lived and peaceable, elephants have roamed the plains and forests of Africa and Asia for centuries, living their complex lives. For much of that time, their interactions with people have been limited—except in Asia, where they were captured and trained to work. But as human populations grow, especially in Africa, the wide, unspoiled lands these giants need to inhabit have shrunk drastically. Pushed back into ever smaller areas—mostly parks—they often find it hard to get enough food to satisfy their enormous appetites.

Worse, worldwide demand for the prized ivory of its tusks has made the elephant a victim of greedy hunters who slaughter it and leave its tuskless body to rot. By 1990, many countries agreed to ban the export of ivory, but poaching (illegal hunting) is still a problem.

Because of hunting and human needs for more land, Africa's elephant population suffered a rapid and alarming decline in the 1970s and 1980s—half of Africa's elephants died. Since then, many programs for saving the elephant have been put in place. But elephants are not out of danger. Continued efforts to protect them are vital, so these playful giants can continue to dwell peacefully on the earth.

Elephants live within a close family structure dominated by the females. The oldest, wisest female—the matriarch—is usually in charge. She is the one who knows where to find water, and what routes to take across the savannahs or through the forest. The rest of the group consists of other females of all ages, along with babies and youngsters. When bulls reach the age of about 15, they usually leave the family to join a bachelor herd of males only. But they continue to associate with the main group.

Rockhopper Penguin

Amazing Feets and Flippers

Most people think of penguins as slow, clumsy animals that are amusing to look at but have no special ability. But if you were to observe penguins in their natural habitat, you might be amazed at what feats they can perform with their ducklike feet and slender flippers. These birds are really all-around athletes, comparable to superb swimmers, racewalkers, and steeplechase competitors.

On the Falklands, South Georgia, and other remote islands that ring the seas just north of the Antarctic Circle, it seems at certain times of year as if the land itself is in motion. A closer look reveals that it is actually alive with penguins—millions of them—waddling about and jostling each other in their crowded colonies, called rookeries.

For though their true element is the sea, penguins must spend time on land in order to mate, lay their eggs, and raise their chicks. The feisty little rockhopper penguin with its spiky crest of yellow and black feathers (and its cousin, the peaceable white-capped gentoo)—come ashore on the sub-Antarctic islands each year to complete this breeding ritual.

The rockhopper's body must function in two very different environments—in the water and on solid ground. That body is round, torpedo-shaped, and compact—perfectly suited for skimming through the seas. Densely packed feathers waterproof them and conceal generous amounts of insulating fat, as well as muscle. Strong, bony flippers propel them efficiently through the water. Short legs with webbed, sharp-

> "**I**n the water, they are sleek athletes, diving 350 feet deep in sub-Antarctic seas or sprinting at speeds up to 17 miles per hour [even faster, we now know]. On land, however, the...birds move with all the grace of short-legged flour sacks."
>
> Tui De Roy

Flippers held out for balance, gentoo penguins run along a beach in the Falkland Islands. They stay close together for protection from the sea lions that prey on them.

clawed feet are positioned well back on their bodies, where they act as rudders for steering.

In many ways, these flightless birds are better designed for the seagoing part of their existence than for life on land. In fact, among birds the gentoo penguin is the world's fastest swimmer, with a top speed of 24 mph for short distances.

And yet, rockhoppers (nicknamed "rockies") make up for their somewhat comical awkwardness on land with remarkable strength and agility. They can cover rough terrain with surprising speed.

Since both species live north of the freezing Antarctic continent, they don't face such extremes of temperature as the emperor penguin. Even so, conditions on islands like the Falklands can be rough. These islands are regularly battered by fierce storms. The land often meets the sea in a wall of rocky cliffs. In winter, howling winds combine with snow and ice to make

Penguins "bodysurf" strong waves right into the rocky shore, and just as the wave breaks, they leap upward and land safely.

the environment even more challenging. But the penguins are built for cold and can swim comfortably through icy water—and even beneath the sea ice, searching for krill and fish to eat.

In the early Antarctic spring (August and September), rockhoppers come ashore onto the beaches and rocks, ready to make their way to their rookeries. When the seas are calm, they often just pop up out of the water, propelled by their powerful flippers, and land squarely on their feet on solid ground. When they come ashore in rough weather, strong winds and crashing surf roll and toss them about, but they still manage to struggle doggedly ashore.

The distance they must travel from shore to their rookeries varies. Rookeries may be far inland—sometimes an hour's trek over rocks and hills. Often the path to them is well worn from years of use. Some rookeries are at the tops of steep cliffs or on narrow plateaus. The penguins' progress over this rough landscape suggests the challenges of the steeplechase, in which people race cross-country over hurdles and water obstacles. The penguins must waddle along, taking short steps and swaying from side to side, sometimes hopping over water, gullies, or rocks.

Rockhoppers are well known for their ability to negotiate difficult terrain. These

Rockhoppers scramble up a steep cliff in the Falklands.

Washed up onto a ledge by the surf, these rockhoppers leap back down to the flat rocks below. "I've seen rockhoppers make jumps off ledges that could kill us," recalls Frans, "yet they just walk away."

plucky little birds stand under two feet tall, but their toughness more than makes up for their small size. While caring for their chicks, rockhoppers may clamber up and down steep cliffs time and again, going back and forth to fish and bring food to their young. They have been seen jumping down off 30-foot ledges and walking away from a fall that could severely injure a person.

Rockhoppers can also be quick on their feet when they need to escape danger. South American sea lions may attack them on the beach, as well as at sea, and the penguins can run astonishingly fast on their short little legs when necessary. A crowd of them, their flippers held out behind them for balance and feet moving double-time, looks somewhat like a group of racewalkers.

Once inland, they are safe from most predators. At their rookeries, they follow a time-honored pattern of breeding and raising young. When they are old enough, chicks leave the nests and gather in a kind of penguin nursery called a creche. This behavior helps to protect the downy chicks from attack by skuas—gull-like birds that are their main enemies at this stage of life. The parents still bring them food, and somehow parents and chicks unfailingly find each other in the crowd with a special call they make to each other.

At last, as the Antarctic summer winds down, the chicks get their adult feathers. Now they are ready to join the adults out at sea, where they will spend most of their lives. Here they can use their bodies in the way that comes easiest to them—"flying" along underwater and "porpoising," or leaping out of the sea across six feet of water to breathe, then reentering without missing a beat.

For now, penguin populations are large, and the remoteness of their breeding and feeding areas protects them from much human interference. But as people encroach more and more on their habitats, as commercial fishing increases and global pollution filters into the fragile Antarctic environment, penguin colonies will have to be monitored carefully, to safeguard the future of this indomitable inhabitant of land and sea.

Writer Tui De Roy describes the scene as rockhoppers climb up from one Falkland Island beach: "Flippers out for balance, they negotiated the easier stretches with a fast waddling walk, but as soon as the going got rougher, they resorted to those incredible leaps that give them their name. In single file they proceeded rapidly up ledges and cornices, scrambling with nails, beaks and flippers over the trickiest bits, occasionally taking backward spills that would make the toughest rock climber think again."

A Parson's chameleon strikes at a grasshopper. It can make tiny
adjustments of its body and tongue at lightning speed.

Chameleon

The Tongue Is Quicker Than the Eye

A cricket sits on a leaf, flexing its wings. Nearly a foot away, a creature like a miniature dragon waits motionless on a tree branch. Its eyes are locked on the cricket in a fixed, cross-eyed stare; its whole body is primed and ready. Suddenly…zap! Faster than the human eye can see, its long tongue shoots out and back again—with the cricket stuck to its tip. The little dragon chews, then gulps, and the meal is finished.

This bizarre and fanciful-looking creature is the chameleon. Found mostly in Africa and Madagascar, chameleons have fascinated human observers for centuries. With its bumpy, varicolored skin and its array of horns, crests, and frills, it really does look like a cross between a dinosaur and a storybook dragon in miniature. And its extraordinary "tongue–eye" coordination enables it to aim as accurately as an expert marksman with rifle or bow.

In the forests of Madagascar, the tree-dwelling chameleon has developed a host of remarkable physical adaptations and special skills for hunting. Unlike many of its fast-moving lizard relatives, who can make a quick dash to snag a meal, the slow-moving chameleon depends on stealth and "concentration" to catch its insect prey. Like a human archer preparing to let fly with an arrow, the chameleon must have its body under absolute control when striking at prey. The insects on which it feeds can hop or fly out of range in an instant. So the

> "Their slowness is something you must witness to believe. The only rapid movement is from the tongue. Even the eyes swivel slowly—the legs and tail move even slower. They fight slowly. Two horned chameleons battling…might take five minutes getting into position, and another five minutes could then go by before one asserted his dominance.…"
>
> Mervin F. Roberts

A grasshopper becomes a meal. Chameleons lack teeth, but strong jaws and digestive juices do the job.

chameleon must approach them undetected, and must stay still and firmly anchored on its branch as it hits its target with pinpoint accuracy.

To remain stable on slender, flexible twigs and branches, the chameleon anchors itself with all four feet as well as with its strong tail. The feet have toes that are opposable (that is, they act like a thumb and fingers to grip a branch). The animal can cling to a branch with such strength that pulling it off by force will often break its legs. Tree-dwelling chameleons have a prehensile tail, like a monkey's, that can be curled around a branch to anchor the lizard when it's ready to strike at prey. When moving along a branch, the chameleon holds its tail out straight for balance.

Like any top athlete, the chameleon is in complete control of its muscles. The creature often rocks back and forth to mimic leaves fluttering in the breeze. As it stalks its insect victim, it may move as slowly as ten steps a minute to avoid being detected. Its walk has an odd, hesitating rhythm as it slowly inches along.

To get insect prey in its sights, the chameleon relies on its amazing eyes. Very large for a reptile, they are set in a dome of skin and covered by scaly eyelids. Each eye can swivel independently, so the chameleon can look all around without moving its head or body.

Once an unsuspecting insect is within range, the chameleon's other unique feature—its tongue—comes into play. This remarkable organ can be extended as far as one-and-a-half body lengths in some chameleons. When it's time to strike, the chameleon suddenly shoots out its tongue by tensing muscles along each side. It can zoom out in $\frac{1}{16}$th of a second—faster than the human eye can follow. A sticky, club-shaped tip grips the prey and reels it back into the chameleon's mouth.

Chameleons are also remarkable in the animal world for their ability to change color. Much of the time they are effectively camouflaged in their leafy habitat by the mottled patterns and colors of their skin. But it's not true that chameleons change color to blend into their surroundings, as many people believe. Rather, color change is usually in response to temperature and light, or to the lizard's own hormones and nervous system.

Because it is a highly specialized hunter that depends on certain plants for the insects that visit them, the chameleon is currently threatened in many places. Stricter enforcement of international laws is needed to protect this unique and fascinating member of the lizard family.

A chameleon hunts from ambush, well-camouflaged in the leafy vegetation.

Leaping Lemurs!

Sifaka and Ringtail

If there were gymnastics contests for animals, the lively, agile lemur would surely be a top performer. All lemurs display remarkable strength and agility in their movements. Some specialize in tumbling and cavorting on the ground, as in "floor exercise" routines. Others hurl their bodies through the trees in tremendous leaps, like trapeze artists or vaulters. Like a human gymnast, the lemur has extraordinarily strong leg muscles to propel its leaps, and strong hands and feet that can grasp securely.

Among the most spectacular leaping lemurs is the sifaka. These furry, brown-and-white creatures are not swingers, like some other primates, but champion jumpers. They use powerful thigh muscles in their hind legs to push off from a tree trunk or branch, and spring across open space with their bodies held vertical, like someone jumping on a trampoline. These leaps can measure up to 30 feet. "Their leaping ability is amazing," Frans Lanting observes, "and they turn themselves around in mid-leap so that their feet face forward to grasp the tree on which they're landing."

Sifakas' feet are large and powerful, perfect for gripping trees. And their long, hooklike hands are made for grasping branches above them, so they can dangle easily. Sometimes they perform a series of leaps, one after another. Frans says, "I've seen them use the forward momentum from one leap and immediately go on to the next one. This use of momentum is probably an energy-saving way for them to get around."

The sifaka is perfectly adapted for a life lived almost entirely in the trees. In fact, Frans says, "Sifakas are so well adapted to the arboreal lifestyle that they can't walk nearly as well as most primates. They have to move with a strange hop—like a little dance—doing everything possible just to stay upright." Often they hop along horizontal branches or sometimes along the ground, their thin, spidery bodies held upright and long arms held up, waving in circles for balance.

In the dry forest of southern Madagascar, Frans caught this sifaka in mid-leap.
It is already turned to face the tree it will land on, paws ready to grasp tight.

The sifaka's feet are made for clasping branches, not walking, so it must hop along on the ground.

The sifaka's cousin, the ringtail lemur, is more at home on the ground, where it finds some of the plants and insects it eats. Still, this alert, active creature with the long, striped tail spends much time in the trees and always retreats to them if it feels threatened. Like the sifaka, it leaps between branches and often runs along horizontal branches on all fours. On the ground the ringtail tends to walk on all fours, too, and can speed up to a gallop.

Lemurs delight in play, and at playtimes they spring and tumble, jump and roll just like the most limber young gymnasts. Frans Lanting describes ringtails at play, "dashing around, doing a lot of crazy stuff just out of exuberance, or in trying out social roles. The young engage in extensive play, chasing each other endlessly during the times the troops aren't moving. Midday is playing time."

These engaging, supremely athletic animals belong to a special branch of the primate family with a fascinating history. All 26 species of lemurs that exist today live solely on the island of Madagascar. Located off the southwestern coast of Africa, this is the world's fourth largest island. Because it is a world isolated from direct contact with the mainland, like Australia, many unique creatures developed here and are found nowhere else—lemurs included. There are no

Ringtail lemurs can move on the ground easily and fast. This baby is barely hanging on.

monkeys on Madagascar; lemurs fill the ecological niche, or role, for primates.

Along with creatures called lorises, pottos, and bushbabies, lemurs are classified as "pro-simians," or "pre-monkeys." This means that they have evolved along a different path than true monkeys. They do share basic primate characteristics—the ability to grasp with their hands, nails instead of claws, and eyes located on the front of their head. But in many details of their anatomy, lemurs are closer to an ancient primate ancestor than to any present-day monkeys. Species range from the tiny mouse lemur, the smallest living primate, to the three-foot-tall indris, a handsome black-and-white lemur that is currently endangered.

Lemurs live in family groups called "troops." Sifaka troops usually contain three to nine animals—males, females, and juveniles. The troop lives and forages within a home range of several acres of forest, feeding on leaves, fruit, berries, and flowers. Sifakas have never been seen drinking water; instead, they get moisture from their food and from licking dew.

Ringtail lemur troops tend to be larger—sometimes up to 30 of them living in a well-organized society. They also spend much time in the trees but, unlike sifakas, they often come down to the ground to eat grasses and other plants, and to parade around and play. They tend to move around more in their home ranges during the day than do sifakas. Both these kinds of lemurs are active only in daytime.

High spirits aren't the only reasons for the lemurs' athletic talents and sociability. They must stay alert and often move fast to avoid falling prey to hawks that patrol the treetops, or to a catlike carnivore known as the fossa. This is another of Madagascar's unique animals, not a real feline but related to the mongoose and civet cat. The lemurs' best defense is to spot the predator before it can get close, and living in groups improves their chances. One or more lookouts will broadcast a long, resonant alarm roar when danger is sighted.

The name lemur comes from the Latin word *lemures*, the Romans' name for spirits of the dead. The lemur's huge, luminous eyes may have inspired early observers to give it this name. Some weird-looking species, like the aye-aye, are nocturnal, and their appearance at night can be ghostlike and startling. Many lemurs also have eerie, moaning calls that echo through the forests of Madagascar—anyone unfamiliar with these sounds could be spooked by them.

Both sifakas and ringtails are highly territorial and will usually chase away other troops that try to enter the territory they have "staked out." Any intruders, human or wild, are loudly scolded. The sifaka actually gets its name from the *shi-fak!* sound it makes when disturbed. Ringtails have a variety of calls. Alison Jolly describes the reaction of one troop as she approached: "…they are already clicking to each other, first one and then a chorus begin to mob you with high, outraged barks. The troop is quite willing to click and bark for an hour at a time in the yapping soprano of twenty ill-bred little terriers."

In more relaxed moments, lemurs enjoy sunning themselves. Ringtails are especially noted for the way they sit up with their knees apart, holding their arms out to the sides or resting them on the tops of their knees—almost like people sunbathing on the beach—just soaking up the warmth of the sun.

Like all primates, lemurs care for their young for a long time. For the first few weeks of life, babies are carried on their mothers' stomachs, but at about three months of age they switch to riding on her back. This may go on for several more months, until the young lemur can get around well enough on its own.

The mother does not change her vigorous lifestyle because of the baby—she dangles upside down in the trees while eating, and leaps from branch to branch as usual. The baby hangs on for dear life, and apparently few infants fall off. Ringtails also carry their babies on the ground, where they may gallop along with the infants astride their backs, looking a lot like jockeys in a horse race.

The lemurs, Madagascar's unique members of the primate world, are in danger in their homeland. Their forest habitat is disappearing at an alarming rate as land is cleared for farming and logging, in efforts to improve conditions for a country whose people suffer from poverty and malnutrition.

Yet scientists and environmentalists recognize the need to preserve what remains of the island's precious natural ecology, and preserves are being set aside. Here, we hope, lemurs can go on living and reproducing so that these gentle and appealing creatures will not die out.

A troop of sifakas in their favorite place—clinging to a tree, with something to lean against.

Elephant Seal

Wrestling for the Top Spot

Every winter, on beaches along the wilder shores of California and Mexico, a kind of wrestling tournament takes place among creatures that weigh more than the average automobile and can "honk" louder than any car horn.

These are the adult males, or bulls, of the elephant seal, largest of all pinnipeds (the marine mammal family that includes seals and walruses). At stake in their contests is a great prize—winners earn the right to mate with females and pass on their genes to future members of their species. Like all their kin, elephant seals spend much time at sea and do all their feeding in the water, but "haul out" on land from time to time—to mate, give birth, and "molt," or shed their fur.

Our California wrestler is the northern elephant seal, surpassed in size only by its cousin, the southern elephant seal, which lives mostly around the islands north of Antarctica. Northern elephant seal males can grow to 15 feet long and reach weights up to two-and-a-half tons, or 5,000 pounds. Females are much smaller, averaging 9½ feet and rarely more than 1,900 pounds.

"**S**ome nose it is, too. About two feet long and as big around as a man's thigh. Not exactly an object you'd want to put in your mouth, although that is what the male elephant seal does when he needs a resonating chamber to amplify his opinions.... The tune is revolting, a combination belch and gag, only in the case of the elephant seal the belch is cosmic and the gag sounds like the Colossus of Rhodes choking on a ham."

Page Stegner

The male is instantly recognizable by his enormous nose, or proboscis, which is elongated somewhat like an elephant's trunk—hence the name "elephant seal." The bull inflates this nose, which hangs down just in front of its open mouth, and produces rhythmic snorts, the mouth cavity acting as a resonating chamber. These incredibly loud sounds carry a clear message—roughly translated as

Evenly matched opponents, two elephant seal bulls bellow threats at each other during their pre-fight ritual.

Except for the bulls' clashes during breeding season, elephant seals live peacefully together in their rookeries.

"I am the greatest!"—to all the other bulls in the neighborhood.

This animal is a good example of what scientists call "sexual dimorphism," which means that males and females of the same species differ strongly in size (or other characteristics), so they can be easily identified. In the seal's case, the vastly greater bulk of the males is a result of the fierce competition they wage over the right to mate. In general, the bigger they are the more successful they will be—a lot like sumo wrestlers.

Bulls also have a shield of very hard skin on their chest and the underside of the neck, a kind of suit of armor to protect them from serious injury during their epic battles.

Like all pinnipeds, elephant seals are adapted to a life partly in water and partly on land. Their streamlined bodies are built for swimming with flippers that provide both power and steering, and they can see clearly underwater.

As mammals that live both in cold water and on sunny beaches, seals must be able to regulate their body temperature (about the same as ours internally). Their short, dense coat of fur helps keep them warm, along with a layer of blubber. Capillary networks in their flippers circulate blood to cool them when they get overheated, and reduce blood flow to conserve heat when body temperature drops. The elephant seal also uses its flippers to throw sand over its body for protection from excessive heat.

These coastal residents keep to the ocean for much of the year. During their ocean forays, elephant seals have been sighted at least 37 miles out from land. The seals feed mainly on squid and fish found at considerable depths—this species is the champion diver among seals, often descending below 700 meters (2,300 feet) and staying down as long as 30 minutes. The only animals that prey on elephant seals are sharks—especially the great white—and killer whales.

Young elephant seal males practice for the real thing in play fights.

Although fairly solitary while at sea, the seals follow a strict social system on land. Males and females of different ages come ashore at different times. The annual breeding cycle starts in early December, when the adult males start arriving at rookery sites to begin their tournament for dominance. One after another, the big bulls confront each other in no-holds-barred contests until a clear ranking order emerges. One bull becomes the "alpha" or top male, who dominates all the other bulls on the beach, with a "beta" male ranking just behind him, and so on down the line.

Frans Lanting, who has observed elephant seals often, notes that the bulls' success in competition depends on several factors—their enormous bulk, as well as timing and psychology. "Timing is critical," he says. "We can compare it with how athletes plan their training to reach peak performance for the Olympics or other important events. For the bulls, mating is their big event. The ones who time their arrival on the beach perfectly, so that they are well fed and in top condition, are the most likely to win battles."

Also like human athletes, some bulls also "psych out" their opponents, Frans believes. The dominant bull projects an image of invincibility with its loud roars, body postures, and other

"Before body contact is made, the bulls threaten each other with an inflated snout, a raised stance, abrupt aggressive movements, and alarmingly boisterous bellows. Only one in 60 of these confrontations gets beyond the threat stage. But if the males are comparable in size, weight and aggressiveness, threats are ignored, the animals square off, and the fighting begins.

"The two behemoths stand chest to chest, feinting and faking, waiting for an opening to fight. Finally, with a fast and powerful blow, one strikes at the neck of its opponent. The attacker's head slashes downward and its sharp teeth rake the opponent's flesh."

Jacques Cousteau

signals. This may explain why one bull backs down from a confrontation for no clear reason, even when both seem well-matched and in good shape.

The adult females arrive shortly after the bulls, around late December, and very pregnant. They gather in groups to give birth within a week after their arrival. Just a few days later, they mate with the bull who has proved dominant in their neighborhood. Sometimes lower-ranking males hang around the edges of the harem and try to mate with females when the boss bull isn't paying attention—but he usually catches on and chases the trespasser away.

Very few males ever reach the status needed to mate with females. In small rookeries, a single male may be the father of all the pups born to the colony. In larger groups, even the most powerful bull can't be everywhere at once, so others may get a chance. The career of an alpha male is short—most hold onto the top spot for only a season, or two at most.

The pups, born right after their mothers arrive at the rookery, nurse for about four weeks and quickly grow to about 350 pounds. They have to take care not to get crushed when the adults roll over—the main cause of mortality in pups. Also, females often attack pups who are not their own. Once they are weaned—around February—their mothers go back to sea. Pups stay at the rookery until April or May, then enter the water for the first time. By then they're extremely hungry!

The elephant seal is a conservation success story. Before the nineteenth century, large rookeries thrived all along the California coast, from Baja to the San Francisco Bay region. But they were hunted so relentlessly for their blubber that by 1900 they were all but extinct—only one group of fewer than 100 animals was known to exist, on Baja's Guadalupe Island. Eventually the seals were protected and they gradually spread northward again, establishing colonies on the Channel Islands off Santa Barbara, then on Año Nuevo, where many people now go to see them in a preserve, under the supervision of rangers. Recently the seals have been showing up at Point Reyes National Seashore, on the mainland about 50 miles north of San Francisco. A real colony is being established there, with more than 250 pups born in the winter of 1996.

Just in the last twenty years, biologists estimate, the total population of elephant seals has grown from 48,000 to more than 125,000. But they still need protection—not just from hunting, but from people getting too close and disturbing them, which often causes females to abandon their pups. Approaching them is also dangerous to human health—the bulls are notoriously bad-tempered during breeding season, and have attacked and injured overly curious observers. These giants are best left alone to conduct their wrestling matches with worthy opponents of their own kind.

At Año Nuevo, a harem of female seals rests while the master stands guard.

Acknowledgments

For their invaluable help in the creation and production of this book, the authors and Walking Stick Press would like to thank: the staffs of Walking Stick Press, Frans Lanting Photography, and Minden Pictures; Tracy Fortini and Georganne Papac of The Nature Company; Jean Lowe and Rick Hill of Andrews and McMeel; Katie Clark of Tien Wah Press; the libraries of the California Academy of Sciences and the University of California, Berkeley; and especially Joanna Lynch. Frans Lanting particularly wishes to thank the researchers and officials who helped him gain access to and understand the wild animals portrayed in this book.